T0288092

Deaccessioned
Landscapes

Deaccessioned Landscapes

Jonathan
Brannen

Chax Press   Tucson 2005

Some of these poems have previously appeared in *Antenym*,
DCPoetry Anthology, *House Organ*, *Juxta*, *Nedge*, *New Orleans
Review*, *6ix*, *Tinfish*, *Unarmed*, *Veer*, *ZYX* and *The Poets'
Calendar* (Sun & Moon Press, Douglas Messerli, ed.).

ISBN 0-925904-34-1

Published by Chax Press
101 W. Sixth Street
Tucson, Arizona 85701-1000

for Cathleen

Memory: 'I see us still, sitting at that table.' But have I really the same visual image — or one of those that I had then? Do I also certainly see the table and my friend from the same point of view as then, and not see myself?

Ludwig Wittgenstein

1

On white november nights they lived
a period of years then left a noisome body
music under the fingernails. Stranger
then strangers the world becomes stranger
the pattern more complicated where blue-eyed
mannequins lie next to the next best thing
next to a circle in a dream of closing.
Symptoms distinguish a bird by its "air"
to "hear" checkerboard buildings where
empty rooms slot the crash of your heart
splashed by the city's disjunctive surf.
I'm swamped every so often which is often
enough. A dark coat floats above the roof.
Languages find a way into one another.

1

empty rooms
place
     semblance

     reinvent
     fallen apart

     no difference
     now
     stars sequestered
     in archaic lyrics
     the earth remembers
     glass
     wind   cold
           nature
                  everything

2

And worlds hang on upwardly mobile trees
moving cursors to previous blanks. To be
high-strung lucky and free comparing people
in parking lots to the symptoms of mad cow
disease is not a new dimension of intimacy.
The swimming word is swimming in a tidal wave
washing away abodes where there's no discernible
discrepancy between bringing down the house
and bringing down the horse. The whole day
was a storybook day bringing posthumous fame
abroad. It was another time's voice a choice
line drawing overwhelmed by an elaborate frame.
The difference between sex and athletics.
Hard-wired fiber optics. The distant rage of tools.

2

shades of blue   exact
             artificial light
   subject
      to
methodologies   across
              cape
      posthumous   sky
                light
                     falls
              room   eyes
      watch   old
                     symptoms
      finding   voices
                        by the wind

3

In an architecture of sound
somnambulant spheres embrace arches
excerpting corridors from enclosed passages.
If time's really an aspect of experience
its serial character is seriously flawed
or characteristically that of an
inclusive series Chinese boxes
Russian dolls or the tubes of a telescope.
From so great a distance the moon's an easy
answer. Many hands are raised in classrooms
like winter wheat waving in spring fields.
Storms blot the day and smudge the night.
Here where weather is the only landscape
I'm swearing off of ordinary letters.

3

place inside space where
all   sides
             structure a line
culminating in a dot
a coat
of unknown
range
        rockets
        in clumsy
                long
                sentences
                a home
                of erasures
                an other

4

O majestic crabs of romanticism
how and in what aspects of the verbal whole
is the author's ultimate semantic
authority implemented? Minus is more exact
than plus. Pure events ground language
because they wait for it as they wait for us
on all the pages that have never been read
on all the blank sheets on a star nailed night.
The voice box is an imperfect structure.
And have they fixed the where and when of it?
The word "flower" applied to a rhinoceros
seems a bit out of place. O pattern of points
when will you finally fill the still white spaces
occupy the vacant slots retrace effaced traces?

4

harder
than verbatim
            motion
                    as factual
                as sleep
            objects
coincide
like water
            rooms
                    where stark light
                disguises
                            streets
                building
                    selves

5

The decorative voice of secret flesh
in darkness where none can tell distances
from differences. The spectrum of grey.
Five shades of blue. The contraction of small
muscles. All eyes ice beneath the arch
of an abbreviated eyebrow
a silent question mark thinking it
counterfeit. What's true of deceleration
is equally true of parallelism.
What requisitions a verity.
Sudden wind abruptly scallops the canal's
surface. Horresco referens I shudder
at the mention yet when you own a mirror
do you then own the reflection within it?

5

serious
        chignon
freeze-framed
stars   violet albedo
      dusty
          in a reality
exterior to
                responsible
                sky   lucid
                isn't the end of
                          always
the future will
                close
                          take meaning

6

Silence sharpened pencils in the street
where mermaids gliding behind windows
are too happy to be afraid. Syllables
govern the world if only for a fraction
of a second. Language is fossil poetry.
To communicate with Mars converse
with spirits like nobody's business.
Just don't say that day is the same as night.
Nothing can come out of nothing. Nothing
can go back to nothing. What passes
perhaps has a passion for passage.
Real life artless and unmetaphored
be mine even if my voice comes from other
worlds like a bird broken by the wind.

6

facts look
     tense

inadequately expressed
accidents
ice howled winds
           need
           white letters

           establish continuity
           confine space

           lull   rough   tracks
           to mine   between knees
           altered states   at the edge
               emerge from emerge
                            address

7

The sky for instance was a damaged canvas
tattered in scattered sunlight. Multi-
encapsulated control diodes
are as clean as a whistle. The moving
accident is not my trade. There are
no chairs in this room. The antique sleep
of prenatal existence where what isn't what
it seems to be. Immensity is the movement
of the motionless. A response isn't
necessarily an answer. Item dissenting
from object. Gravel roads are deceptively simple.
Ears of corn. Visual fields. Vestigial tails.
Virtual realities. You who are reading
over my shoulder *wait a minute!*

7

art   tepped   ide   avern nd sa
ow   th ba   ca   et ou a d ink
   artender sked   hink ot   esc
pli   en e isappeared   oes rasing
n il gible nam   tual
   st tute erasu   lect th est
swer rom   hoices ovided elow:

A

        B

                C

                        D

                                E

   ny   srooms re lik
in   cab   routing   a field

Another thing I rarely mention is how
I used to wake up screaming as a kid.
Snatches of sentences occur on both tongues
as if to say life's a struggle that deserves
a better cause. Either you recognize yourself
in the world or you don't. Either way you can
never know exactly what time it is
but in sleep you have no age. Here it is
nature that imagines. The working drawing
of a shape. A sequestered jury
of unfashionable furniture
compound interest and sophisticated
teenagers. Untelevised the triple chin
of happiness lights up the late night page.

       dust
     an old   in
translation   part   loss
carried   camera bag lotto
waking   afternoon
mouthed   simple fractions
   complex fractures trace   cracks
     in winds   place   next
        to a house   blinds
                              air
          photographs
          jury
              stones
          than remembered

9

Fish are not imprisoned souls seven years
in the flood and I'm at the mercy of no one
but myself. Could a phone call to New York
convince you that the earth exists? The phone line
is cream. Some stories are a part of something
larger. Some are fragments apart. Lately
I've been thinking how little identity matters
that the idea of eternity has its roots
in death. Carrier pigeons through jet engines
are crude but efficient redefinitions
of flight. I don't yodel even when every-
thing else fails. This is a brief cameo
in the interior distance. The way
snowflakes turn sunlight or sunlight bends rain.

9

so often pictured
        crashing
in regions
rainfalls usually
            verb situations
            selves arrange
            wetware recollapsing
            zero
            necropolis
                        protocol
emptied   buffaloed
confusion stuns eye
vocabulary   the body
to see the voice   speaking

Trigue terval cluded stigate. Don't let
the darkness catch me here. Sometimes
evenings are one of the Fine Arts.
Sometimes mis amigos are looneytoons.
Of a given space in a given time
of the taken place in taken time
memory tricks the inelegant heart.
Writ in moods recalled in sounds so familiar
that they're only noticed in their absence
friends have died too soon. Nothing can fill space
abandoned. The sky above the roof
is waiting for you outside the occurrence
of this discourse. Sweating out the night.
Thinking back to myself remembering.

each place
sculptural
in the swim

       things
       object

postulate
where

    time   places
             only
             night
             structures

each instance is
damaged   in tattered
     starlight   harangue

On the verge of blubbering some dark
maternal secret while waiting for the light
to change people still prefer talking to
their cars to the stormy boredom of home
for the holidays. Painted over Pepsi
signs are altogether indifferent.
Deaccessioning landscapes things are getting
serious. Limits imitate limits.
Trees cresting hills can't create the perfect climate.
Blind leaves by dry roads where fathers spit
stop coddling yourself. A peculiar
dialectic in space persists. My grandfather
dead before I was born. Black and white photographs.
A color detached from the idea of color.

11

words   haunt   echoing
in breath   sky   imprecise
                             sun
reconstituted
too hot
        to touch
        in the warm
                we're all ears
                certain
                  impossible
           a dog
           sneezed
           brooding about being
                        an aspect of experience

Misquoted gestures. Disheveled stars.
Snugly cloistered I think about endless space
in abbreviated sentences. Not one begins:
"The woman in question." Disproportionate trees
skirt the disappearance of chrome fenders
where seasons are apt and the spectrum isn't
the issue. Let's not be in too big a hurry.
One size does not fit all. Let's go back
to where W.C. Fields lies dreaming of orange groves.
This isn't everything but like everything
it seems so. When in a sequel you might learn
anything but then again. It's a day
at the beach a line drawn in the sand. The night
transparent without external reference.

dying
ebb and flow
     space formed out of
     an idea represented
     unforeseen worlds
     nature   our eyes
     the way   form
     absences   distances
     progress   cut
     signifying   want
     misplaced displaced
           here
           place not from
           the contract
                 of sleep

Theories of representation in fields
of potatoes. Frescoed ceilings noon the edge.
The impossible opposite of gestures
where musical chairs yield less ingenuous
devices. Consider this unsaid
the sky's been overcast since morning.
The much from than is the where and how of it.
Behind the window it takes the place of captioning.
Is this the same as knowing? Hope is retarded.
Memory becomes separation.
Overqualified underemployed needing
a solution and needing it now.
Habitable space. The struggle of people
to realize themselves in such times as these.

13

what   things   used to mean
breezes   life
past   change
isn't
our lives
        dictate   thought
                sequence
                what
                words don't mean
                fire
                building
                the sky
                        in action

                  until the fall

Everything matters. Temperature changes.
Now the sky's pale blue almost pigeon down grey.
Wind rules these ruins in the evening.
Silencing words a detail overwhelms
the entirety the way telling fingerprints
mar glossy black and white photographs.
In a wilderness of mirrors I feel like
a walking blender mixing strange concoctions.
It imagines a space to fit its proofs.
Balance is the triumph of place. The motion
is tabled. The table depicts nothing.
A spoke from the wheel on which silence is broken.
Tightening roots are unintelligible
to the wind. Grey does not equal gray.

everything I know
as soon
to ground
these tales of water
what water can see
a sad
ness
as usual
possible
events
fly
one wing
future   mapped
memory   present

Nothing useful is of lasting value.
Canceling canceled images conceding
dialogue with eyes across undiscovered
places. Love becomes conspiracy theory.
The verb to be. And thy cheek unprofaned
by tear at this intersection of
erasable roads. A nervous chronicle
which like a shark contains a shoe.
A meaning without future or past.
Objects that never surrounded me
living in the same room twice
with fictions I needed to believe.
Fugitive moments in scoured terrain.
Instead of new words a new hermeticism.

leaf or blossom
lost   beneath
sites of future   sentences
slang
    ate definitions   sphere
    deputized   nights and days
    socks lack
    locks are cross
    in these parts
    thing   other
    languages want   languages die
                   of or for
                   the want of words

    to speak

A handkerchief is nothing like a wing.
Budge red clump stars. Snow white among white dwarves.
Unsplotched. It's a terrific afternoon.
Data memorizes you. The flight
of stairs and not a cloud in the skies.
A million miles away a hill plus
or minus a dimension. These words
are identical with words of a language.
Do you dream of silk scarves with red hexagons?
Stepping back in amazement your footprint
is as delicate as an animal's
flounced whorled undulating denticulated.
There is no end to longing. A row
of white letters. The line of the horizon.

time   territories
beyond   time   shift
light falls
          inventing
          archaic lyrics
                    from this
          fugitive phenomena
     closets   mirror   doors
       photograph   in
          languages   into
     another in the republic
     of
        the
             executed

Believe you me the instinct for self-
preservation is no myth. My hands are
becoming forgetful and I'm given
to fabrication. Words generalize.
Everything's covered up with patches cut
from its own cloth. This person had probably
been a number of places that day.
My pronouns are waiting. Rain is wet.
The wind is born in the mountains and comes
down to the sea. What common language
unravels the motives of objects
the object of motives the something you can't
afford not to know? If you believe in words
I know a confusion of sky and it is gorgeous.

didn't unimaginable
night sleep
in and out language
          which language
          dreams into memories
     the present
     torn
     cinematography
              as artificial light
              drifts
              time is
              quiet
              through a break
              clouds haunt us

A spoon is a spoon. Art isn't a spoon
but this is debatable. Light becomes color
in painting and space the holes in hollowness.
Pieces have been replaced by degrees.
The reality behind a muggy afternoon.
Obsessive behavior is more complex
than you might expect. A mental filing system.
The way flowing water catches the light.
A shock of hair. The alphabet is a
short dictionary of the spatial world.
At this unique distance from isolation
fucking sounds like flip-flops on a muddy path.
How I wish now I could invent a brand
new color just for you to daze the night.

like time
          in abandoned
          magnolias
phonemes
          wick light
          from rooms
ravels
unravel
          black nights
          night sweats
                              rain
                              drops
                              splat on
                              dry glass

Facing the parenthesis you inhabit me.
The sky for instance was a damaged canvas
representing the way something is happening.
The match m ignited at time t.
Lit from within a dust of colored
perceptions falls on a black backdrop
as with a thud or joyous commotion
about a woman beautiful as she bends
her hair sweeping away the should of usually.
The future is inscrutable. The air's
different now. Tiny rooms in huge houses.
T   e   h   o   i
  h   w   y   f   t
and that one perfect word.

instead
of flying
        in musical terms
        empty words
            where this
                    "happened"
        impossible
        letters traffic
                    in syllables
                    unutterable
                            tonight
                    sculpts sleep
                            standing
                            in darkness

O Rogue Elephants of Innovative
Technologies rampaging through the future tense
inside the Cow Palace where cold doth not sting
the grass green of the green grass has been revoked.
Full of parrots the fog disperses
milky in the spring grotto where stones fatten.
In a given time of a given space
tables and chairs must feel out of place.
Objects articulated for action
waiting to occur. On the face of it
the whole hurly-burly of human behavior
connecting nothing with nothing.
Intersecting streets which no longer exist.
A map of erasures. Means to an end.

the terrain dreams
of criminals
      the process of
      history tongues
           the quiet sea
    writing a counterpoint
    passing
        angles leaning learning
    the world
    telling stories only told
           so many
           litter a landscape
           starkly stumbled
                  upon

The terrain is impossible. The dreams
of criminals come alive inseparable
from the process of realization.
The history of tongues is the first drops
of night rain falling into the quiet sea
writing a counterpoint to illness.
Life is a fragile and passing thing.
In odd corners leaning at odd angles
learning to see the world late night groups
of two or three are telling stories only told
after so many drinks. Odd numbers litter
a landscape with starkly emerging methodologies
just waiting to be stumbled upon.
The sequence of events. The event horizon.

21

rogue
technologies
tense inside
        grass-green
           parrots
            spring to
   tones   in time
        tables and chairs
articulated
for action
face
   human behavior connecting
        streets which exist
               as erasures

Understand the terms arrived at
are symptoms also. That it is ill-advised
to hear smells and cover yourself in pitch
like a feline mummy. That there are no
empty words just as there are no empty rooms.
The place where this "happens" is the color green
though clearly this is chronologically
impossible. So many capital letters.
Traffic's heavy tonight and the sky hangs low
over the great brouhaha. Syllables are
envelopes containing letters. Unutterable
dreams. On late night tv tonight Alaskan
Eskimos are racing kinetic sculptures.
Nonallegorical cows sleep standing in darkness.

the damaged
parenthesis
representing
time
      ignited
      perceptions
      sweeping
            away the
            future of
            tiny rooms
        in
        the why
        of it
            on hwy one

Architects didn't design you
unimaginable as the night
when you lie sleeping dreaming in and out
of language. All memories are in
the present the way snowflakes turn sunlight
or shadows map torn paper.
The cinematography of sleep
is as precise as artificial light.
Penitent seasons are locked in absence.
Anecdotes drift in fixed ideas.
Everything is the gestures of jugglers
in a posthumous text. Women wearing
loose cotton warrant quiet celebration.
Daylight breaks through. Words come back to haunt us.

a spoon is a spoon   is   a spoon
           light
           painting space
           by degrees
  reality
      is more
      than you might expect
          flowing waves
        alphabet the days
  short
      distancea
      flip-flop
             now now can invent
               the night

When you sleep dreaming in and out
of language what language do you dream into?
Magnolias pin abandoned divas
to telephones while heifers stand like statues
in a farm field bordering a lake where
half-sunken boathouses contemplate what
the wind might do. Memory mirrors
the size of night singing tint to the horizon.
Living rooms are alive with conversation.
She's wearing black tights and an oversized
sweater. Nested eggs in a trance.
Individual raindrops go splat
on the windshield each leaving a tiny
island of wet on the dusty glass.

instinct is myth   hands are
                  forgetful
      given
      words
      covered with passion
             a person
     places that
             pronoun
     waiting is born
     common language
     unravels objects
     the object   the object of desire
                the something
                      you believe in

Time has no significance in these territories
beyond the time it takes the wind to shift.
Light falls from her breasts to her thighs.
Face to face inventing with moistened fingers
culling archaic lyrics from this double
current of fugitive phenomena
inside that nest where birds startle into flight.
So many closets with mirrored doors.
Sleepless photographs. Another winter
sweated out while languages find a way
into one another. In the republic
of letters articles of mind are putting
spokes in the wheels of your unspoken thoughts.
The well-executed turn of phrase.

                              like a wing
budge red clump stars   among white dwarves
  splotched   a terrific afternoon
         memorizes   flight
   stairs and
         miles away a hill
   minus a dimension
                   of language
          scarves
               your footprint
          delicate as an animal
               undulating
               end to longing
        letters   line   the horizon

Bush-league towns that neither leaf nor blossom.
News of lost continents sunken beneath
seas and of the sites of future sidewalks.
Suicide by self-fascination.
Trial by fire. Trial by phone tag. This sphere is
the deputized checker-board of nights and days.
Your shirt and socks (the black silk ones with golden clocks)
have been seen crossing the plains on a bicycle
seeking the great perhaps. Speech situates
the self in relation to the other.
Life they say in these parts is one damn thing
after another. Sensations words and
memories continually derail
trains of thought. Everything is distance.

canceled images
conceding dialogue
undiscovered places
conspiracy theories
     verb unprofaned
     at this intersection of
     erasable chronicles
which contains
a meaning
   future or past
       objects living
       spaces   fictions
   to believe
       scoured in words

Dying which truly evolves from life. Ebb and flow.
Fixed shadows. A black and white photograph.
The space formed out of a space.
The way an idea is represented
in an unforeseen light. Worlds without
signatures and pictures before our eyes.
The way form defines formlessness.
The absences of absence. The distances between.
Signs of progress and cut-rate haircuts
signifying whatever you want them to.
Misplaced and displaced here is a place
that I'm clearly not from. It's come to this now.
The contraction of small muscles.
The cinematography of sleep.

misquoted gestures
cloistered
in abbreviated sentences
in disproportionate
questions
        chrome fenders sleep
        the spectrum isn't
        in a hurry
                lies dream
                everything
                but a sequel
    day
                drawn in   and
                without   reference

Is time really an aspect of experience?
Words come back to haunt us re-echoing
in the breathless sky as imprecise
as cantaloupes asleep in the sun.
"Oranges and lemons," say the bells of Saint
Clements. "Reconstituted or squeezed freshly?"
ask the bells of Saint Presley too hot to touch
in the warm Memphis sun. On the porch
we're all ears. Green is green and doing
is doing and what is certain is certain
because it's certainly impossible.
Throw out the much of muchness. A dog has fleas
say the bells that just sneezed to keep it
from brooding about being a dog.

               verge
           in unison
     talking   cars
     stormy   home for
            signs
indifferent
landscapes
imitate limits
           create   perfect climate
           roads   where
                     odd
                     dialectic space persists
white photographs
                     the idea of color

Here is a place that I'm clearly not from
a sculptural win-win situation.
Getting back in the swim of things
an article a noun the object of a verb.
Semblance lumbers in winter postulations
but where does the truth lie?
Sometimes it seems in some places
a hop-skip away. Sometimes a leap
of faith. A star nailed night. The voice
is an imperfect structure. A torn
landscape. The sky for instance
was a damaged canvas scattered in tattered
starlight. To swell the night's harangue
amid realistic orioles I hammer home.

                    spirit
                            cluded
stigate   darkness   here
            is
    time is
            space in
                        memory
                recalled
                        absence
too soon   space
abandoned sky
                        outside the occurrence
                        outside the night
                        remembering

Dissolution is often pictured
as a wave of terror crashing against
sea strangled sands. In regions of abundant
rainfall the soil is usually acidic.
You can verbally rearrange situations
which in themselves would resist rearrangement
a sort of wetware tsunami recollapsing
the universe to zero as easily
as a cat in a necropolis
rearranges priorities. Emptied
buffalo herds push the wind. Confusion
stuns the eye. The emphatic silent
vocabulary of the body. To see
the voice of words speaking in signs.

imprisoned
in
   myself
       stories
          a part
              fragments apart
identity matters
          the idea roots
               through
                    redefinitions
        every
           thing fails
              every
                distance turns

There's a duster that attracts dust
like a magnet an old world rug in a
modern translation a book in three parts
a loss carried forward. Camera bag lotto.
Waking from a short afternoon nap cotton-
mouthed and cotton-headed amid simple fractions
and complex fractures a tracery of cracks
in a windshield replacement shop next door
to a house with drawn blinds stuffed full of over-
stuffed armchairs and dried starfish. A sleepless
photograph. Another thing I rarely mention.
A jury of furniture. A drawing of
fig-shaped stones on a street not unlike
brevity though smaller than remembered.

another thing
is how I used (up)
snatches of sentences
       tongues
    deserve
  recognize
know
exactly what time it is
  no age
     sequestered
       unfashionable
       and
         triplicate
         night page

Descartes stepped inside a tavern and sat
down at the bar. "Can I get you a drink?"
The bartender asked. "I think not," Descartes
replied, then he disappeared. Does erasing
an illegible name actually
constitute erasure? Select the best
answer from the choices provided below:

A. A shared secret is still a secret.
B. Speech is a boundary separating humans
   from other species.
C. A shared secret is no longer secret.
D. Speech is a boundary that separates nations.
E. Nationalism is a failed experiment.

Many hands raised in classrooms are like
winter wheat waving in spring fields.

              damaged
           sunlight

   clean as a whistle

      in this room
                  where
what isn't

what
     is
        deceptively
                    simple
          visual fields
vestigial
         reality
      over   a minute

33

What do artifacts look like once one has quit a place
inside the future tense where cold doth not sting?

1. Inadequately expressed in mathematical terms.
2. Industrial accidents.
3. Ice howled winds.
4. I don't need it, I don't want it, I don't get it.
5. Rows of white letters.

Q. Comparison establishes continuity, is continuity
    odious?
    Please confine your response to the space provided.

A.   *As one careens from lullabies through soundtracks*
        Trying to determine the difference between knees and needs
        Before arriving at altered states of experience at the edge of death
        The denouement emerges from the emergency
        And one perceives illness as a kind of state-of-the-union address.

silence
       behind
       syllables
             a fraction
             a second
             language
       to communicate

       day   as night
             nothing
       back to nothing
       passage

             voice
             other
                  worlds

The woman with the serious face
her hair pulled back in a chignon
a freeze-framed breast revealed lit by evolved
stars and the ultraviolet albedo
of the moon on a dusty road only
the earth remembers is in a reality
exterior to this one a French billboard
promoting responsible mammography.
The winter sky is lucid with cold
but this isn't the end of the world
and what actually happens is always
so far in the future that you will
never get close enough to know its true
appearance. To grasp words. To take meaning.

           secret
                distances
         spectrum
             grey
                   contraction

   abbreviated
 silent
             deceleration

   requisitions
sudden
wind

  the mention
        the reflection
           within

The couch is harder when I can't sleep
than verbatim parentheses inside
the persistent motion of doing
as lawless as treasure as factual
as chairs. The antique sleep of prenatal
existence. The object of desire.
A coincidence of walls rises up
like water from the ground in the cadenced
structure of rooms where stark light is stored
white in addiction. Becoming disguises.
Vast clown armies are taking the streets
miming a feeling that's felt to be missing.
Are buildings huge models of themselves? Words are
cages. The voice of thought thinking itself through.

a e i o
how   what aspects
        u
authority implemented minus
        events ground language
        for it
    pages
    blank sheets on
        an imperfect structure
        the where and when of it
the word
        out of place
                    still white spaces
                        effaced

A place is resting beside the space where the
small brass key resides. Inside the dictionary
of symbols this structure a line
culminating in a dot represents
a coating of ice a miscarried fetus
of unknown sex a disposable short-
range antitank device. In this book
I have a rocket launcher to aid
my progress in clumsy traffic on
intersecting streets leading nowhere.
Snatches of sentences. The future
they say is a home equity loan.
A map of erasures. One damn thing
after another. Limits imitating limits.

singing
an architecture
somnambulant
numbers
breath
serial
flawed
boxes
tubes   scope
distance
raised
winter   in a field
blots   day   smudges   night
wearing   letters

Day in and day out the difference between
sex and athletics extends beyond
the abuse of irony into the misuse
of the ironic. In artificial light
experimentally naive subjects
wishing to approach us with emerging
methodologies stumble across the checker-
board landscape of day and night bringing
posthumous fame abroad. The sky's disfigured
torn by nails where light falls through opening
doors to the next room in the eyes of those
I watch. Maybe they're only symptoms.
Languages finding a way. Fossil voices
from broken worlds spoken by the wind.

worlds hang

                  blanks to be
       and
       lots to   symptoms
             word
       tidal
abodes where   no
       between   down
and   day
was   posthumous
         time
            frame

        optics
           the distant

Here there are no empty rooms
just as there are no empty words.
The place where this "happened" is retarded
still hoping some semblance of center
will hold. It's the wheel that's intact
as well as its reinvention.
The revolution has long since fallen apart.
There's no difference now between life and weather
here where the cow-eyed stars sequestered in the night
cull archaic lyrics only the waning earth
remembers. Collapsed to zero.
A tiny island on dusty glass.
Trial by wind. Trial by cold. Trial by
the problematic nature of everything.

white
period
music under
then   world becomes
                    where
          next to the next
next   circle   closing
          in   air
to hear   buildings
empty rooms
                 under
          every which
                         way into
                         another

The circle breaks as the plane lands
in the eyes of those I watch. The spectrum
of grey. Obsessive pronouns writing
what the wind might do. Signs signifying
whatever within an inclusive series
of endless spaces the room races
to believe in. Odd angles among red
hexagons as inscrutable as damaged
memories on torn canvas. A sad business.
An aspect of experience employing struggle.
Transparent gestures instead of a new
hermeticism. The air is different now.
Snatches of sentences and that one perfect word.
A row of white letters is no end to longing.

word   cages
  sushi bars
     schizoid
          distance
    memory tricks
         icons
   glyphs   deciphered
   wind rules
     the darkness   here
       night thinking back
        remembering
          lies
            to
              come

Drawing a blank nothing resembles anything
at all though clearly smaller than recalled
thinking back to myself remembering.
Articles of faith. The word washes away
inseparable from the process
of realization. Eternity
is rooted in closure next to a circle
in a dream of death retracing effaced
traces. Lost continents. The site of future
metaphors. Displaced distances
are misplaced in sleep. A black and white
photograph taken before I was born.
Time detached from the idea of color.
Minus is more exact than plus.

cinematography   unfolds
ravels
      of light
      a quiet
             empty
drawn   blind   cells
cities   rivers
           direction
      blue   red yellow
      name   edge
      to write   out
      the whole
        air thick
          with rain

The pattern becomes more illegible
each time it's redrawn. Sketchy memories
overwhelmed by memory's elaborate frame.
The hurly-burly of intersecting perceptions
crisscrossing the scraped surfaces of the painting.
Captive light torn open to daze the sight.
The place where this "happened" is the color green.
There are no empty canvases
just as there are no empty rooms.
To experience vertigo when looking out
an apartment window but not when looking
out the window of a plane. It's its own
evidence. So many capital cities.
So many unutterable dreams.

41

dream mechanisms
articulate
process
      cultures fast-forward
infinity's
a second
unpunctuated
diminishing
        raw
        zed   nought
time   fiction   events
described here   appear
        imaginary
            day was day

The convocation of skin in nocturnal
climates when the question of surfaces
arises. Face-to-face with moistened fingers
retracing a map of erasures
the geography of the body becomes
a literary conceit a landscape
with starkly emerging methodologies
merging within cloistered space in
abbreviated sentences. Not one begins:
The contraction of small muscles is reinventing
the wheel. All space is socially articulated
and vulnerable to manipulation.
The winter sky is lucid. You will never
get close enough to know its true appearance.

42

memories
of
        objects
  speak
        to thought
                exhaling
                    haunted by
            time is   debris
            extinction's
            romantic
            gesture   gestures point
                        to   the idea
                              roots in
                                    matter

To voice intentions the spectrum of grey
has been replaced by degrees. You rack
your brains when memory fails but then
you fall into a sequence of thoughts
as inclusive as a series of Chinese
boxes or Russian dolls scattered about
a terrain the wind has rearranged
or refuses to abandon. The floor
beneath the chair beside the table
against the wall. Gaps between memories
are named history. Though it be jade
it crumbles. Though it be gold it breaks.
Though it be feathers of quetzal
it tears and fragments in time.

faces
  close
    to know
      their true appearance

      leave
     without   words
  mouths
realizations   the fallen dance
                each act
                    unfound
            separate
    carrying forever
migrations   of the circle
where is what   so long ago

Blind words linger half-spoken in half-starved
shadows like lotus pods left on a bus seat
inside a plastic sack. Big city small talk
reveling in the unexamined life.
The undiluted sequence of events
is as vivid and violent as any
Tarantino film. Discolored curtains
frame the window almost by accident.
Glued to the loopholes form can't announce itself
without also announcing the formless.
A quintessence. The seeming of the room.
The politics of neglect. Seized by an
uncertain wind the rain speaks a foreign
language. The world about us.

meanings
to grasp   grip
  what   seems   you
  in   are   in
pain   that
 of light   surface   erased by
  can't be   self
   sky   low over
     turns   out   leaves   hand
      light   is seen   weather
    disorder
    serious face   before
   born statues in a field
          or passage

You can verbally rearrange meanings
to grasp situations to come to grips
with what it seems you really aren't up to.
Paintings that are paintings and not paintings
of paintings. Paintings that are paintings
of light. The surface is erased by
what can't be recalled including the self
and the sky slung low over the great brouhaha.
The glove turns inside out as it leaves the hand.
In deficient light sleep is seen as Seasonal
Affect Disorder. The woman
with the serious face dead before
I was born. Statues in a field. What passes
perhaps has a passion for passage.

word
pods
        small talk
the unexamined
sequence of events
is a
    film
frame   almost by accident
      loopholes form
  without
  form
    the
      uncertain wind the rain speaks
        the world about us

Two faces turn to face you in a dream
so close that you will never get far enough
away to know their true appearance.
What I believe I believe. What we
believe we leave unsaid unable
to say it without putting words in
the mouths of others. Vestigial
realizations. The fallen dancer
slipped on air. Fast forwarded. Each act
flies out of death. Facing west from unfound
old waves house maternity. To separate
an hour carrying forever. Land of
migrations shores of the circle
where is what I started so long ago?

to voice
has been replaced
memory fails   you fall
into a sequence of thought
boxes or
            the terrain searching
            the situation
            beneath beside
                    against
                    between contents continents
                    named history
                                    crumble
                    feathers
                            fragment   the wind

Hushed contemplation beckons memories
of articles elapsed. Parts of speech
and bits of objects beneath a scrapnelled sky.
To speak is an act of faith the conversion
of thought. Faith which doesn't doubt itself
is no faith at all. Exhaling deficiency
manifold doohickeys are haunted by
outmoded anguish. Time is close. Its debris
asphyxiates in extinction's ageless night.
O majestic pronouns of romanticism
your sweeping gestures point out fictions
I and I once needed to believe. That the idea
of identity has its roots in death.
Lately I've been thinking how little matters.

                    skin
climates   surfaces
                    finger
            erasures
    geography   becomes
            a landscape
            emerging
            snugly
cloistered
in sentences
            contraction
            is reinventing
            winter sky
            to know its true appearance

The dreams of mechanisms are criminals
articulated for action separated
from the process of realization.
Relativistic cultures fast forward.
Infinity's a two-way street and *you* are
the second person trying to get across.
Unpunctuated desires punctuate
diminishing shelf-lives. Exclamation
points. Raw data. Troubling statistics.
Life has become a zed and two noughts.
Time is a work of fiction. The events
described here including the appearance
of Willard Scott are purely imaginary.
The whole day was a storybook day.

48

illegible
time
frame
       intersecting
       perceptions
              captive light
              places
                     color
              rooms
              looking out
              apart
                     it's its
                     evidence
                     unutterable

49

The cinematography of sleep unfolds
in the ravels of the mind. A painting
of light. A black and white photograph.
A quiet celebration of women wearing
loose cotton. The bed is empty in the house
with drawn blinds where cells are fields perhaps
whose cities rivers and seas assign
a different color to each direction
north white south blue east red west yellow.
All have the same name at the edge of the
prairie. I wanted to write about you
and by implication the whole universe
instead of soggy birds in air thickly
grassed with rain. Hope is retarded.

49

nothing resembles
all
recalled
     articles
         inseparable
         from
         closure
         in
           traces
           of future metaphors   distances
                                                        sleep
                                                       before

           time detached

                                                      the idea of

Words are cages of illusions.
A sushi bar in Elbow Lake is merely
a banal schizoid episode a brief
cameo in the interior distance
where memory tricks the inelegant
heart. Stick-figure icons are no stone
whose glyphs have never been deciphered.
Wind rules these ruins at evening.
Don't let the darkness catch me here
sweating out the night thinking back
to myself remembering. Let's go back
to where W.C. Fields lies dreaming of orange groves.
Grey does not equal gray. To speak is
an act of faith. Words come back to haunt us.

the circle breaks
the spectrum
    obsessive pronouns
            signs signifying
    within
   endless spaces
         angles among
              damaged
              memories
     experience
    transparent gestures
             hermeticism
             snatches of sentences
             a row of letters   longing

Recent Books from Chax Press

David McAleavey, *Huge Haiku*
Norman Fischer, *Slowly but Dearly*
Nick Piombino, *Hegelian Honeymoon*
Jerome Rothenberg, *A Book of Concealments*
Bill Lavender, *While Sleeping*
Elizabeth Treadwell, *Chantry*
Allison Cobb, *Born Two*
Beverly Dahlen, *A-Reading Spicer & 18 Sonnets*
      (New West Classics 3)
Todd Baron, *TV Eye*
Karen Mac Cormack, *Implexures*
Pierre Bettencourt, *Fables*
Heather Thomas, *Resurrection Papers*
Keith Wilson, *Transcendental Studies* (New West Classics 4)
David Bromige, *As in T As in Tether* (New West Classics 2)
Nathaniel Mackey, *Four for Glenn*
Charles Bernstein, *Let's Just Say*
Hank Lazer, *Deathwatch for My Father*
Robert Creeley, *Yesterdays*
Mark Weiss, *Figures: 32 Poems*

For additional titles please visit our web site:
      http://www.chax.org